The Cultivational Planner

A DEVOTIONAL PLANNER FOR WOMEN
Establish. Cultivate. Create.

"The Cultivational Planner: Devotional Planner for Women"

Copyright © 2020 by Jenny Erlingsson

All rights reserved. This book is protected by copyright laws of the United States of America. This book may not be copied or reprinted for commercial gain or profit. The use of short quotations is permitted and encouraged. Permission will be granted upon request.

Scripture quotations marked (NIV) are taken from the Holy Bible, New International Version®, NIV®. Copyright © 1973, 1978, 1984, 2011 by Biblica, Inc.™ Used by permission of Zondervan. All rights reserved worldwide. www.zondervan.com The "NIV" and "New International Version" are trademarks registered in the United States Patent and Trademark Office by Biblica, Inc.™

Scripture quotations marked (NLT) are taken from the Holy Bible, New Living Translation, copyright ©1996, 2004, 2015 by Tyndale House Foundation. Used by permission of Tyndale House Publishers, a Division of Tyndale House Ministries, Carol Stream, Illinois 60188. All rights reserved.

Scripture quotations marked (ESV) are from the ESV® Bible (The Holy Bible, English Standard Version®), copyright © 2001 by Crossway, a publishing ministry of Good News Publishers. Used by permission. All rights reserved.

This book is available at: www.milkandhoneywomen.com and some online retailers
Cover & Interior Design by Jenny Erlingsson via CANVA

Reach us on the Internet: www.milkandhoneywomen.com
ISBN TP: 978-1-7346780-6-2

For Worldwide Distribution, Printed in the United States of America
1 2 3 4 5 6 7 8 9 10

The Cultivational Planner
Establish. Cultivate. Create.

This Beauty Belongs to:

Name:

Contact Info:

Journal Start Date:

www.milkandhoneywomen.com

Welcome to Your
Cultivational Planner

Yes, I know. the word "Cultivational" may be the cheesiest thing you've heard in a while. But it is the best way to describe what this is. It is your tool for inspiration, devotion, cultivation & motivation.

If you are like me, you are often toting multiple books and notebooks in your devotional time with the Lord. Jotting down thoughts in your journal, copying Bible verses, making a grocery list, setting an appointment, etc. With this planner, the goal is not to multitask your spiritual life with Christ but to make every moment matter. **To make your planning purposeful.**

So here is something that I hope assists you in all you do. it is a planner, journal and devotional book all in one. The Cultivational planner is designed to help you cultivate a deep Rooted and well rounded relationship with Jesus and to not forget the things he reveals. The best plans are made with Him.

Core Components

- **ESTABLISH:** Grab your Bible and spend some moments reading a short devotional that will plant seeds of Christ-Centered Identity, Intimacy & Influence in your life. Take time to reflect and write what the Lord speaks to you.
- **CULTIVATE:** Throughout the week you'll see verses from the Bible, reminders to pray, to give thanks and to keep cultivating a life of devotion.
- **CREATE:** Keep track of those important things like To-Do's, grocery needs, appointments and other random tasks. In all of it, keep your heart centered on Christ so that *what* you do overflows with His love and joy.

Cultivational Planner

- **Monthly Calendar:** There are 6 blank monthly calendars at the beginning of the planner. This allows you to not be limited by year. Just fill in the right dates and jot down those important moments.

- **Divided by weeks:** The Cultivational is divided into 26 weeks that should cover approximately 6 months. Each "Establish" devotion starts off a new week. The Cultivational logo ⓒ is placed at the beginning and end of each week's pages as a reminder.

- **Plan Your Day:** Each day has half a page dedicated to it. Instead of hourly times, the days are divided into morning, afternoon and evening blocks. This takes the pressure off your planning, keeps your work flowing and allows you to prioritize sections of your day. If you have a specific appointment or meeting just write that time into the related section. (i.e 12:30 lunch meeting written into the afternoon section)

- **Be creative:** The sections for lists and writing responses are whatever you want to do with them. You can decide when you need a grocery list, packing list or list of your favorite songs. You may want to purchase stick on dividers or use a book mark to help you differentiate your months or weeks if you choose. You can print off a FREE BOOKMARK AT WWW.MILKANDHONEYWOMEN.COM. At the back of the planner are more journal pages for you to dream, create and plan with.

All right friend, get on with the cultivation!

I'm that girl.
tapping your shoulder from behind,
whispering in your ear "You can do this."
I'm that girl.
who believes the little things matter and our
frustrated places can become sacred spaces where
we sacrifice our will for His..
I'm that girl.
who always believes there is more. Who refuses to
take moments at face value but searches for the
eternal value in each happening.
Let's be those girls.
Ashy, calloused praying knees, who help their
sisters in this fight to keep on shining.
Shining bright, building up an inferno in the night.

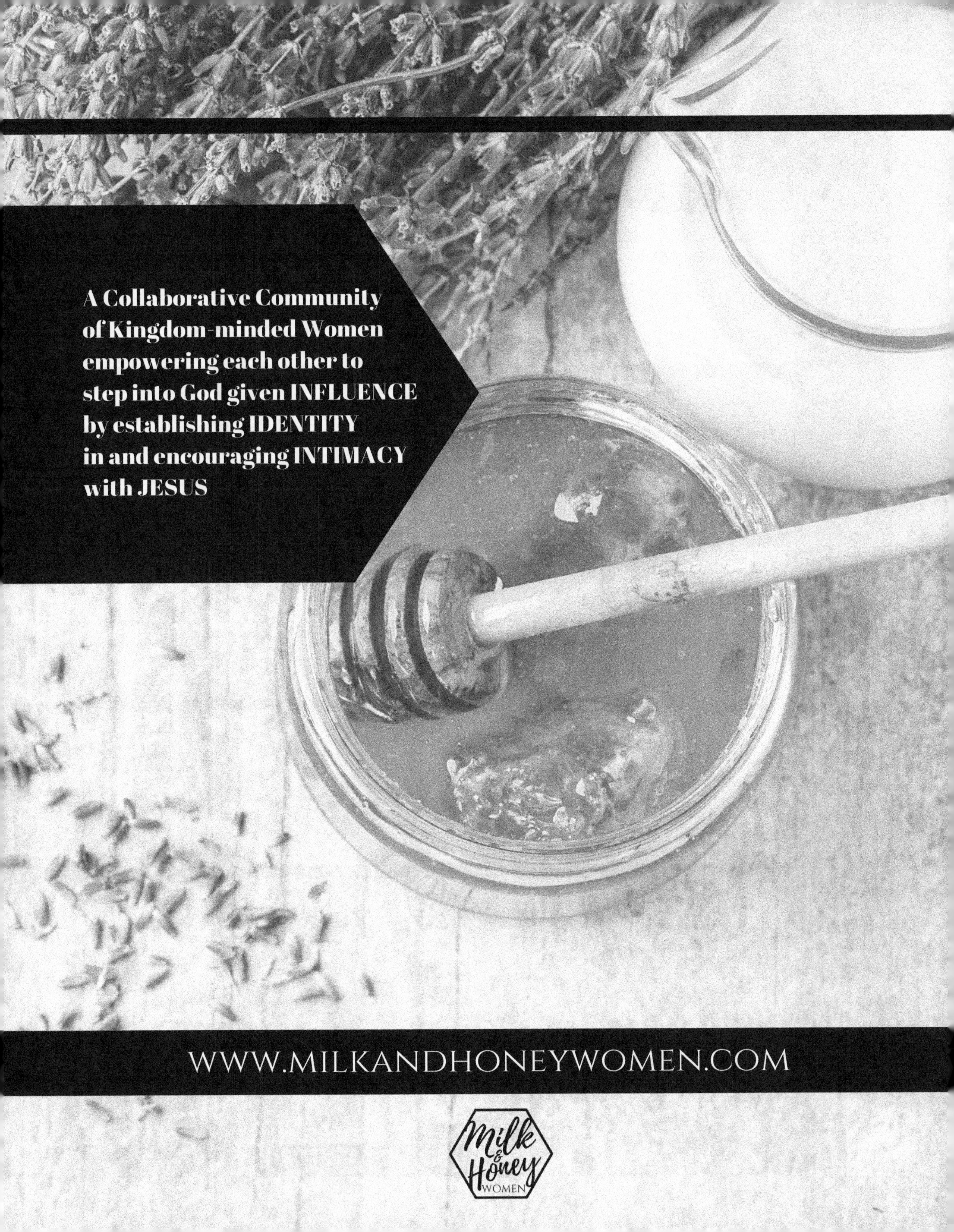

A Collaborative Community of Kingdom-minded Women empowering each other to step into God given INFLUENCE by establishing IDENTITY in and encouraging INTIMACY with JESUS

WWW.MILKANDHONEYWOMEN.COM

Monthly Calendar

MON	TUE	WED	THU

Month

FRI	SAT	SUN	Notes

Year

Monthly Calendar

MON	TUE	WED	THU

Month

FRI SAT SUN Notes

Year

Monthly Calendar

MON	TUE	WED	THU

Month

FRI	SAT	SUN	Notes

Year

Monthly Calendar

MON	TUE	WED	THU

Month

FRI	SAT	SUN	Notes

Year

Monthly Calendar

MON	TUE	WED	THU

Month

FRI	SAT	SUN	Notes

Year

Monthly Calendar

MON	TUE	WED	THU

Month:

FRI	SAT	SUN	Notes

Year

WEEK 1 — Establish

"Chosen"

> "See how very much our Father loves us, for He calls us His children, and that is what we are!"
> 1 John 3:1a NLT

God chose us. Created us from the dust of the earth out of the overflow of his loving heart. Made in the image of His beautiful face. He formed us to operate with Him. To steward creation. Trusting us to cultivate each moment into something that reflects his nature and gives Him glory. When we choose to be chosen, confess our sins and receive the gift of salvation offered to us by Jesus, we are now co-heirs with Christ. We are born into a new kingdom and given an eternal family. He calls us His children, breaking us from every lie, accusation and belief that tells us that we don't belong. The kingdom is about family. You have a part to play and a Father to lean on. We are a church beautified and empowered by the Holy Spirit, the gift and deposit Jesus released to us as He returned to the Father. A promise of what is to come and the source of an abundant life.

What does it mean to you to be chosen?

Reflections

_____
_____
_____
_____
_____
_____
_____
_____
_____

Month of:

Important This Week

- ◯
- ◯
- ◯
- ◯
- ◯
- ◯

Create ♡ Meal Ideas

Monday

☐ morning

••••••••••••••••••••••••••
afternoon

••••••••••••••••••••••••••
evening

Tuesday

Create ♡ List it Out

morning

afternoon

evening

Milk & Honey
For Your Heart

"So, you have not received a spirit that makes you fearful slaves. Instead, you received God's Spirit when He adopted you as His own children. Now we call Him, "Abba, Father."
Romans 8:15 NLT

Wednesday

Cultivate

morning

afternoon

evening

Mid-Week Reminder

We know we are chosen but how does that relate to the day to day? Being sure of who we are and who we belong to should produce confidence in us. Should eliminate the fear. Giving us the stability we need to choose well in all that we do.

Honest Thoughts

Thursday

morning

afternoon

evening

Friday

morning

afternoon

evening

Cultivate

BEING LOVED

Saturday

morning

afternoon

Don't Forget to take time to Rest

evening

Sunday

morning

afternoon

evening

Random Thoughts

WHAT IS CURRENTLY ON YOUR MIND?

Cultivate Prayer

Cultivate Gratitude

Create ♡ Notes & Hopes

WEEK 2 *Establish*

"Not Alone"

"I will not leave you as orphans; I will come to you." John 14:18 NIV

At times the hustle and bustle of our lives will try to dictate to us the lie that we are the ones that need to remain in control. If we want something to happen it won't get done unless we do it. And slowly we pull away from the intention of God's heart, building our tower of babels in different areas of our lives. But we can make a better choice. We can choose to do this differently. Decide that we want to be in true relationship with the One who loves us best. The One who has the ability to give you what you need for what He has made you to do. You can choose to be chosen. You don't have to do any of this alone. You can lift your eyes and set your face on Jesus, who is always making His way towards you.

Reflections

_____
_____
_____
_____
_____
_____
_____
_____

Month of:

Monday

morning

Important This Week

- ◯
- ◯
- ◯
- ◯
- ◯
- ◯

afternoon

Create ♡ **Meal Ideas**

evening

Tuesday

morning

afternoon

evening

Create ♡ List it Out

○
○
○
○
○
○
○
○
○
○
○
○
○
○
○
○
○
○
○
○

Milk & Honey
For Your Heart

"Let us then approach God's throne of grace with confidence, so that we may receive mercy and find grace to help us in our time of need."
Hebrews 4:16 NIV

Wednesday

Cultivate

morning

afternoon

evening

MID-WEEK REMINDER

How does viewing God as your true Heavenly Father shape your communication with Him? Children don't usually have boundaries when they approach their parents. Those of you with young kids know that for them there seems to be no place off limits (i.e. can I use the bathroom privately please?!) Through Jesus we have been given access to the throne of God, to go to Him boldly, as His beloved children.

Honest Thoughts

_____
_____
_____
_____
_____
_____
_____
_____
_____
_____
_____
_____
_____

Thursday

Friday

morning

morning

afternoon afternoon

evening evening

Cultivate
BELONGING

Saturday

☐ **morning**

· ·
afternoon

Don't Forget to take time to Rest

· ·
evening

Sunday

Cultivate Prayer

morning

afternoon

evening

Cultivate Gratitude

Random Thoughts

WHAT IS SOMETHING FUN YOU DID THIS WEEKEND?

Create ♡ Notes & Hopes

WEEK 3 — Establish

"Formed"

> "When I consider your heavens, the work of your fingers, the moon and the stars, which you have set in place, what is mankind that you are mindful of them, human beings that you care for them?" **Psalm 8:3-4 NIV**

Do you ever consider the raw and intimate way we came into being? Mankind, the pinnacle of his creation? Formed and breathed into, breathed into and formed. Man from the dust and then breath. Breath and then woman from the dust of man's flesh. Humanity held and formed in the hands of the Creator, stooping low to delicately form us in his image and then coming face to face with us in order to breathe his breath into us. I think about this a lot. Such an intimate wind runs through our bodies. Carrying oxygen to brighten our blood, giving us the strength and stamina we need to run and pursue all that we've been given stewardship over. Breath and blood entwined and intermingled. Breath at creation, blood at the cross, breath in the Great Commission. Carrying the presence of the Holy Spirit to fill our lungs, brighten and highlight the blood shed that cleanses us from all sin. The breath of resurrection power giving life to our bodies and the stamina and strength, power and boldness to run the race that we've been given to run. Take a moment to focus on Christ. Breathe deep. What thoughts come as you do?

Reflections

_____
_____
_____
_____
_____
_____
_____
_____
_____

Month of:

Important This Week

-
-
-
-
-
-

Create ♡ Meal Ideas

Monday

☐ morning

• •
afternoon

• •
evening

Tuesday

Create ♡ List it Out

morning

afternoon

evening

Milk & Honey
FOR YOUR HEART

"And with that he breathed on them and said, "Receive the Holy Spirit".
John 20:22 NIV

Wednesday

Cultivate

morning

afternoon

evening

MID-WEEK REMINDER

Today. This week. You have what you need to keep on going, to carry through. Knowing Christ means that we have been given the Holy Spirit. Sent to us to bring comfort, equipping, teaching, boldness, power and love. When you feel alone, or unprepared or confused, take a moment. Breathe in deep and remind yourself of who dwells within you and of the solution that He brings.

Honest Thoughts

_____
_____
_____
_____
_____
_____
_____
_____
_____
_____
_____
_____
_____
_____

Thursday

morning

afternoon

evening

Friday

morning

afternoon

evening

Cultivate
YOUR VALUE

Saturday

☐ **morning**

• •
afternoon

Don't Forget to take time to Rest
• •
evening

Sunday

morning

afternoon

evening

Random Thoughts

WHAT IS ONE PLACE YOU WOULD LOVE TO VISIT?

Cultivate Prayer

Cultivate Gratitude

Create ♡ Notes & Hopes

WEEK 4 - Establish

"Breath"

> "Then the Lord God formed a man from the dust of the ground and breathed into his nostrils the breath of life, and the man became a living being."
> **Genesis 2:7**

Let's think about this even more. He started us with breath. The Holy and divine filling our lungs with the presence of Himself. Sealing our value with the kiss of his eternal inspiration. The air of his essence permeating our lungs and sending supernatural oxygen into every part of our DNA, marking us forever as His. Formed. Created. Chosen. The presence of the living God, bringing life and animation to simple clay. Sparking our hearts with the imprint of the divine. He reached down to kiss us and release in us inspiration.

We are no more than dust and clay if we are without his breath in our lungs. What he declares over us is the fuel that we need to keep in motion our movements. We must breathe in deep of the song God sings over us. Take in the melody of the master artist so that we can set a rhythm that sends ripples all around, shifting atmospheres and cutting off roots where they are found. What in your life this week needs the breath of God on it?

Reflections

_____
_____
_____
_____
_____
_____
_____
_____

Month of:

Important This Week

-
-
-
-
-
-

Create ♡ Meal Ideas

Monday

☐ morning

••••••••••••••••••••••••••
afternoon

••••••••••••••••••••••••••
evening

Tuesday

Create ♡ List it Out

morning

afternoon

evening

Milk & Honey
For Your Heart

"So God created mankind in his own image, in the image of God he created them; male and female he created them.'"
Genesis 1:27 NIV

Wednesday

Cultivate

morning

afternoon

evening

Mid-Week Reminder

It's hard at times to look in the mirror and see ourselves as Image-bearers. Maybe life's circumstances or our own choices have altered our physical bodies beyond our desire. Yet when we know Christ, we are seen through a different light, illuminating even more how valuable we are. It's that value that brings the right motivation to take care of this temple we've been trusted with.

Honest Thoughts

_____
_____
_____
_____
_____
_____
_____
_____
_____
_____
_____
_____
_____

Thursday

morning

afternoon

evening

Friday

morning

afternoon

evening

Cultivate
YOUR SURROUNDINGS

Saturday

☐ **morning**

• •
afternoon

Don't Forget to take time to Rest

• •
evening

Sunday

morning

afternoon

evening

Random Thoughts
WHAT MADE YOU SMILE THIS WEEK?

Cultivate Prayer

Cultivate Gratitude

Create ♥ Notes & Hopes

WEEK 5 *Establish*

"Declare"

> "They triumphed over him by the blood of the Lamb and by the word of their testimony
> Revelation 12:11a NIV

There is a strong voice within you. It is made even more potent and impactful by the journey that you've been through. We overcome and see triumph take place over the enemy of our souls when the blood of Jesus and those words of our stories mingle and intertwine again and again. We were not meant to be silent, we were not meant to hold back. We were meant to speak out and declare, operating as our Father does. The manner of your speaking and the sound of your voice may differ from others. It may not sound like the person next to you. But it is meant to be released nonetheless. Even the softest whisper, overflowing from an abiding heart, can shake the foundations, can make walls crumble. What walls need to crumble in your life? In the lives of your family?

Reflections

_____
_____
_____
_____
_____
_____
_____
_____
_____

Month of:

Important This Week

- ⬡
- ⬡
- ⬡
- ⬡
- ⬡
- ⬡

Create ♥ Meal Ideas

Monday

morning

....
afternoon

....
evening

Tuesday

Create ♡ List it Out

morning

afternoon

evening

Milk & Honey
For Your Heart

"Sing, barren woman, you who never bore a child; burst into song, shout for joy, you who were never in labor; because more are the children of the desolate woman than of her who has a husband," says the Lord."
Isaiah 54:1 NIV

Wednesday

morning

afternoon

evening

Cultivate

Mid-Week Reminder

Our voices are not only relevant when we accomplish something great. They are not only necessary after the win happens. No. Sometimes we have to shout out before we receive what we are praying for. At all times, we should lift voices in thanks, preparing our hearts to trust God even amidst the seasons we feel empty and lacking. He values that voice of faith and it always produces fruit.

Honest Thoughts

Thursday

morning

afternoon

evening

Friday

morning

afternoon

evening

Cultivate
YOUR ROAR

Saturday

☐ **morning**

• •
afternoon

Don't Forget to take time to Rest
• •
evening

Sunday

Cultivate Prayer

morning

afternoon

evening

Cultivate Gratitude

Random Thoughts

WHAT SONG MOVES YOU DEEPLY IN THIS SEASON?

Create ♡ Notes & Hopes

WEEK 6 Establish

"Inheritance"

> "By the word of the LORD the heavens were made, their starry host by the breath of his mouth."
> Psalm 33:6 NIV

When you operate in your inheritance as sons and daughters of God, you come into agreement with the One who the Bible says "breathed out the stars". How incredibly powerful is that? This same breath that sent stars and solar systems and galaxies hurtling into space, bent down so low, so personally, so intimately, to breathe that same creative breath into you. He didn't stop it at creation. He didn't stop it at the Great Commission. He continues to call out, coming near, ready and willing to breathe in us and empower us with his Holy Spirit. He is the one that originated the breath in you, therefore he must remain the continual source of what we take in. What creative solution is waiting on you to embrace and release?

Reflections

_____
_____
_____
_____
_____
_____
_____
_____
_____

Month of:

Important This Week

- ○
- ○
- ○
- ○
- ○
- ○

Create ♥ Meal Ideas

Monday

morning

afternoon

evening

Tuesday

Create ♥ List it Out

morning

afternoon

evening

Milk & Honey
For Your Heart

"Therefore go and make disciples of all nations, baptizing them in the name of the Father and of the Son and of the Holy Spirit, and teaching them to obey everything I have commanded you. And surely I am with you always, to the very end of the age."
Matthew 28:19-20

Wednesday

Cultivate

morning

afternoon

evening

MID-WEEK REMINDER

We have permission to speak because we were first spoken to. What we release is not merely random words. Our voices being released are in response to the one who loved us first. It is an act of worship that comes from the overflow of the Lord's work in our lives. As we ourselves release our breath and raise our voices we then become the literal inspiration for others to do the same.

Honest Thoughts

_____
_____
_____
_____
_____
_____
_____
_____
_____
_____
_____
_____
_____

Thursday

Friday

morning

morning

· ·
afternoon afternoon

· ·
evening evening

Cultivate

YOUR ACCESS

Saturday

morning

☐

....
afternoon

Don't Forget to take time to Rest
....
evening

Sunday

morning

afternoon

evening

Random Thoughts
WHAT BROUGHT YOU JOY THIS WEEK?

Cultivate Prayer

Cultivate Gratitude

Create ♡ Notes & Hopes

WEEK 7 — Establish

"Speak"

> "Then Deborah said to Barak, "Go! This is the day the Lord has given Sisera into your hands. Has not the Lord gone ahead of you?" So Barak went down Mount Tabor, with ten thousand men following him." Judges 4:14 NIV

When you speak, walls come tumbling down. When you release a shout in the time that's ordained for you, strongholds can't stand against the power in a voice that's in agreement with the Lord. God's Word in us gives the power to our voices, running through our vocal cords, sending vibrations that release tones and timbre to our unique sound. When Joshua and the Israelites obeyed the strategy of the Lord they came into agreement with His victorious plan. Speak sister, don't be silent, release what's been entrusted to you. What kind of instruction or strategy has the Lord given you lately for a certain situation?

Reflections

_____
_____
_____
_____
_____
_____
_____
_____
_____

Month of:

Monday

morning

Important This Week

- ◯
- ◯
- ◯
- ◯
- ◯
- ◯

•••••••••••••••••••••••••••
afternoon

Create ♡ Meal Ideas

•••••••••••••••••••••••••••
evening

Tuesday

morning

afternoon

evening

Create ♡ List it Out

Milk & Honey
For Your Heart

"When the trumpets sounded, the army shouted, and at the sound of the trumpet, when the men gave a loud shout, the wall collapsed; so everyone charged straight in, and they took the city."

Joshua 6:20 NIV

Wednesday

Cultivate

morning

afternoon

evening

MID-WEEK REMINDER

Your voice is more powerful than you think. We forget that at times when we let negativity and gossip color our tongues, painting pictures that are not accurate or affirming. Yet when these rapid fire weapons of ours are in alignment with the Word and Spirit of God, we release words and prayers and messages and encouragement that moves mountains large and small. The question is, do you believe it?

Honest Thoughts

_____
_____
_____
_____
_____
_____
_____
_____
_____
_____
_____
_____
_____
_____

Thursday

morning

afternoon

evening

Friday

morning

afternoon

evening

Cultivate
YOUR CONFIDENCE

Saturday

morning

afternoon

Don't Forget to take time to Rest

evening

Sunday

morning

afternoon

evening

Cultivate Prayer

Cultivate Gratitude

Random Thoughts

WHAT IS YOUR FAVORITE TREAT?

Create ♡ Notes & Hopes

WEEK 8 Establish

"Sweetness"

> "He said to her, "Daughter, your faith has healed you. Go in peace and be freed from your suffering."
> Mark 5:34 NIV

I believe it's a season where the Lord wants to lavish his love on you. He wants to woo and make whole his church. He wants women who will saturate their surroundings with his presence, who ooze his extravagant love and therefore love supernaturally. But this can't happen if we are leaky vessels. If there is a hole or wound somewhere that is causing what he pours in to get lost within our hurts and disappointments and frustrations and rejections and pride and insecurity. He wants to love you to wholeness. He cares for what you care about and wants you to know who you are in Him. What is heavy on your heart right now that you need to put in the arms of your loving Savior?
(excerpt from Milk & Honey in the Land of Fire & Ice)

Reflections

_____
_____
_____
_____
_____
_____
_____
_____
_____

Month of:

Important This Week

-
-
-
-
-
-

Create ♡ Meal Ideas

Monday

morning

··
afternoon

··
evening

Tuesday

Create ♡ List it Out

morning

afternoon

evening

Milk & Honey
For Your Heart

"For the LORD your God is living among you. He is a mighty savior. He will take delight in you with gladness. With his love, he will calm all your fears. He will rejoice over you with joyful songs."
Zephaniah 3:17 NLT

Wednesday

Cultivate

morning

afternoon

evening

Mid-Week Reminder

It's easy for us to get wild and crazy over our favorite thing. Maybe its a movie you've been wanting to see, a new phone, or an upcoming trip. At times we let those things lavish us with so called "love" instead of positioning ourselves before the one who loved us first and loves us well. He cheers for you, dances over you, sings songs of crazy joy over you. What will be your response?

Honest Thoughts

_____
_____
_____
_____
_____
_____
_____
_____
_____
_____
_____
_____
_____

Thursday

morning

afternoon

evening

Friday

morning

afternoon

evening

Cultivate
YOUR IDENTITY

Saturday

morning

afternoon

Don't Forget to take time to Rest

evening

Sunday

morning

afternoon

evening

Random Thoughts

What is something that made you laugh this week?

Cultivate Prayer

Cultivate Gratitude

Create ♡ Notes & Hopes

WEEK 9 *Establish*

"Sweet Spots"

"As the Father has loved me, so have I loved you. Now remain in my love. If you keep my commands, you will remain in my love, just as I have kept my Father's commands and remain in His love. I have told you all this so that my joy may be in you and that your joy may be complete." **John 15:9-11 NIV**

You may hear the term "sweet spot" used when someone is really in their element. They are in their perfect role and their efficiency and effectiveness is at its peak. But this is usually temporary because components may shift that keep that sweet spot from being consistently activated. However, there is opportunity for all the children of God to be in a permanent sweet spot. The pressure is not on us to make it happen but it is our choice to position ourselves in the flow of God's love. Digging deep to allow our roots to reach water that never runs dry. Letting it flow up through every area of our lives, providing the sustenance for fruit to grow no matter the season. Even when the landscape around you seems bleak and dry, maybe you are being positioned to release what will nourish, speak and release life over yourself and others. What does it look like for you to anchor yourself in Christ?

Reflections

_____
_____
_____
_____
_____
_____
_____
_____
_____
_____

Month of:

Important This Week

- ⬡
- ⬡
- ⬡
- ⬡
- ⬡
- ⬡

Create ♡ Meal Ideas

Monday

morning

....
afternoon

....
evening

Tuesday

morning

afternoon

evening

Create ♡ List it Out

○
○
○
○
○
○
○
○
○
○
○
○
○
○
○
○
○
○

Milk & Honey
For Your Heart

"For I am convinced that neither death, nor life, nor angels, nor principalities, nor things present, nor things to come, nor powers, nor height, nor depth, nor any other created thing, will be able to separate us from the love of God, which is in Christ Jesus our Lord.
Romans 8:38-39 NIV

Wednesday

Cultivate

morning

• afternoon

• evening

Mid-Week Reminder

"Nothing is more likely, nothing more effectual to revive the drooping spirits of the saints, than to be assured of God's love to them."
Matthew Henry Concise Commentary*

Are you sure of God's love for you? Even in the seasons where you don't feel like you are doing much for Him? Are you confident enough to still position yourself near Him?

Honest Thoughts

_____
_____
_____
_____
_____
_____
_____
_____
_____
_____
_____

*Peabody, MA : Hendrickson Publishers, 1996

Thursday

morning

afternoon

evening

Friday

morning

afternoon

evening

Cultivate
YOUR SWEET SPOT

Saturday

morning

afternoon

Don't Forget to take time to Rest

evening

Sunday

morning

afternoon

evening

Random Thoughts

WHAT IS THE LAST MOVIE YOU'VE SEEN THAT MOVED YOU?

Cultivate Prayer

Cultivate Gratitude

Create ♡ Notes & Hopes

WEEK 10 *Establish*

"Fragrance"

"But Jesus, aware of this, said to them, "Why do you bother the woman? For she has done a good deed to Me." Matthew 12:10 NIV

The fragrance of Mary's extravagant worship changed the atmosphere around her according to John 12. A fragrance that blessed the heart of Jesus, a fragrance that filled the room. It even ruffled a few feathers. But Mary did not have to fear. Jesus covered her. In this story we see that ultimately we are not responsible for the outcome but we are responsible for our obedience This is what happens when daughters know who they are, know their position and know how to be intimate. How to love their Savior and themselves well. When you do these two things, love the Lord your God…and love you neighbor as yourself…you can't help but bring change. He truly wants you to become and be His. So what are the things keeping you from being that? Ask Him, even now.

Reflections

_____
_____
_____
_____
_____
_____
_____
_____

Month of:

Monday

morning

Important This Week

-
-
-
-
-
-

afternoon

Create ♡ Meal Ideas

evening

Tuesday

morning

afternoon

evening

Create ♡ List it Out

○
○
○
○
○
○
○
○
○
○
○
○
○
○
○
○
○
○
○
○

Milk & Honey
For Your Heart

"I AM THE LORD'S SERVANT," MARY ANSWERED. "MAY YOUR WORD TO ME BE FULFILLED."
LUKE 1:38 NIV

Wednesday

Cultivate

morning

afternoon

evening

MID-WEEK REMINDER

Have we made room in our life for the things God wants us to say yes to? Are we setting a rhythm of asking his opinion when we set our schedule? Do we even know the words he speaks over us so that we can obey his plan for our lives? It is in those moments of obedience that we get to experience the abundant life promised. We won't have to schedule it in.

Honest Thoughts

_____
_____
_____
_____
_____
_____
_____
_____
_____
_____
_____
_____
_____

Thursday

morning

afternoon

evening

Friday

morning

afternoon

evening

Cultivate
YOUR FRAGRANCE

Saturday

morning

afternoon

Don't Forget to take time to Rest

evening

Sunday

morning

afternoon

evening

Random Thoughts

What do you prefer?
Candles or essential oils?

Cultivate Prayer

Cultivate Gratitude

Create ♡ Notes & Hopes

WEEK 1 — Establish

"Loved in Detail"

"When Jesus heard what had happened, he found the man and asked, "Do you believe in the Son of Man?" The man answered, "Who is he, sir? I want to believe in him." "You have seen him," Jesus said, "and he is speaking to you!"
John 9:35-37 NIV

Jesus doesn't just want you healed, he wants you whole. The Bible has numerous accounts of how Jesus approached the needs of people. The woman with an issue of blood needed to be reminded of her identity as a daughter. The blind man who was healed and then rejected needed to be reminded that he did indeed belong. God is interested in breaking the box of your perception, of your control, of other people's rejection. He sets you in a wide place of freedom, no longer limited by the labels of your circumstance. And he digs deep, healing the wounds we hide from the sickness that seeped in. He loves us in detail, so specifically and intricately. Is there an area that needs to be loved to wholeness in your life?

Reflections

_____
_____
_____
_____
_____
_____
_____
_____
_____

Month of:

Important This Week

- ⬡
- ⬡
- ⬡
- ⬡
- ⬡
- ⬡

Create ♡ Meal Ideas

Monday

☐ morning

• •
afternoon

• •
evening

Tuesday

Create ♡ List it Out

morning

afternoon

evening

Milk & Honey
For Your Heart

"The thief comes only to steal and kill and destroy. I came that they may have life and have it abundantly."
John 10:10 ESV

Wednesday

Cultivate

morning

afternoon

evening

MID-WEEK REMINDER

You were not just meant to survive. Jesus promised an abundant, satisfying life. It doesn't mean that there will not be trouble in this world. But what it does mean is that we have access to an abundance of love, peace, joy, confidence and immeasurably more. Circumstances may try to dictate our feelings but they cannot dictate who Jesus is.

Honest Thoughts

_____
_____
_____
_____
_____
_____
_____
_____
_____
_____
_____
_____
_____
_____

Thursday | Friday

morning

morning

afternoon | afternoon

evening | evening

Cultivate
YOUR PLACE

Saturday

☐ **morning**

• •
afternoon

Don't Forget to take time to Rest

• •
evening

Sunday

morning

afternoon

evening

Random Thoughts
WHERE DO YOU GO WHEN YOU NEED A BREAK?

Cultivate Prayer

Cultivate Gratitude

Create ♡ Notes & Hopes

WEEK 2 *Establish*

"Wilderness"

"Therefore, behold, I will allure her, and bring her into the wilderness, and speak tenderly to her. And there I will give her her vineyards and make the Valley of Achor a door of hope. And there she shall answer as in the days of her youth, as at the time when she came out of the land of Egypt."
Hosea 2:14-15 ESV

The Lord desires to lavish his love on you and wants you to experience the overflowing fullness of it. Even when you have walked through those hard times and places, the Lord will make a way to draw you out and close to himself. He just may be bringing you to a place to speak to you, without distraction. To remind you again of his promises, of his thoughts over you. He sets your identity, he reveals his nature, he heals your heart. Don't despise the wilderness season, but open yourself up to all that he wants to do in you while you're there. We can all go deeper. We can all move closer. What is God pulling out of you as He pulls you in?

Reflections

_____
_____
_____
_____
_____
_____
_____
_____
_____

Month of:

Important This Week

-
-
-
-
-
-

Create ♥ Meal Ideas

Monday

☐ morning

••••••••••••••••••••••••••
afternoon

••••••••••••••••••••••••••
evening

Tuesday

morning

afternoon

evening

Create ♡ List it Out

Milk & Honey
For Your Heart

"Who is this coming up from the wilderness leaning on her beloved?"
Song of Solomon 8:5 NIV

Wednesday

Cultivate

morning

afternoon

evening

Mid-Week Reminder

Every woman encounters wilderness seasons. It's inevitable. But there is beauty found in those places. Not because its easy or everything lines up the way we want it to. But because God is there. And its in those moments, the distractions are less and we can't help but fix our eyes on Jesus. He may do some pruning and cutting and stripping of the things you've held on to, but even if you come out limping, you come out leaning on Him.

Honest Thoughts

Thursday

morning

afternoon

evening

Friday

morning

afternoon

evening

Cultivate
YOUR TRUST

Saturday

morning

afternoon

Don't Forget to take time to Rest

evening

Sunday

morning

afternoon

evening

Random Thoughts

WHAT IS YOUR DREAM ROLE/CAREER?

Cultivate Prayer

Cultivate Gratitude

Create ♡ Notes & Hopes

WEEK 3 *Establish*

"Connection"

"I have entered my garden, my treasure, my bride! I gather myrrh with my spices and eat honeycomb with my honey. I drink wine with my milk. Oh, lover and beloved, eat and drink! Yes, drink deeply of your love!" Song of Songs 5:1 NLT

We all want something tangible, something that we can touch, taste and feel. But how many times do do we get disappointed with the outcomes of our cravings? The word says to fix our eyes on the unseen. There are moments where God leads you to places where that's all you can do. There is nothing else to put your eyes on but Him. To see him as he is, to remember what he has done, to be aware of how much you are loved. In those moments the tangible is made manifest from the intangible. The promised provision of his presence, the milk and honey for your soul is poured out. He provides a sweet spot of communion and connection you can rest in. Sit before the Lord, even for just a few minutes. Write down what He speaks to you.

Reflections

_____
_____
_____
_____
_____
_____
_____
_____
_____

Month of:

Monday

☐ morning

Important This Week

- ⬡
- ⬡
- ⬡
- ⬡
- ⬡
- ⬡

•••••••••••••••••••••••••
afternoon

Create ♡ Meal Ideas

•••••••••••••••••••••••••
evening

Tuesday

Create ♡ List it Out

morning

afternoon

evening

Milk & Honey
For Your Heart

"You have captured my heart, my treasure, my bride. You hold it hostage with one glance of your eyes, with a single jewel of your necklace. Your love delights me, my treasure, my bride. Your love is better than wine, your perfume more fragrant than spices."
Song of Songs 4:9-10 NLT

Wednesday

Cultivate

morning

afternoon

evening

Mid-Week Reminder

True love originates from the creator of love himself. The biggest romantic gesture was carried out when Father God allowed his Son to come to earth, carry the cross and pay the price that we never could. He did so in order to pay the price for the church, his beautiful Bride. You may be longing for romance and/or true love in your life through a spouse, children, or even deeper friendships. Be reminded today that you have someone in your corner who sees you, knows all of you, and calls you to come and experience His love.

Honest Thoughts

_____
_____
_____
_____
_____
_____
_____
_____
_____
_____
_____
_____
_____

Thursday

morning

afternoon

evening

Friday

morning

afternoon

evening

Cultivate
TRUE LOVE

Saturday

☐ **morning**

••••••••••••••••••••••••••••••
afternoon

Don't Forget to take time to Rest
••••••••••••••••••••••••••••••
evening

Sunday

morning

afternoon

evening

Random Thoughts

WHAT IS YOUR FAVORITE RESTAURANT?

Cultivate Prayer

Cultivate Gratitude

Create ♡ Notes & Hopes

WEEK 4 — Establish

"In His Shadow"

> "Those who live in the shelter of the Most High will find rest in the shadow of the Almighty. This I declare about the Lord: He alone is my refuge, my place of safety; He is my God, and I trust Him." Psalms 91:1-2 NLT

Rest is a valuable commodity. If you're a business leader, an entrepreneur, a minister or a full-time work at home mom, you know that rest can be few and far between. Sometimes the nature of our assignments don't leave much room for us to be still. But there are times we run frantically out in the open, trying to make things happen, exposing ourselves to the elements in our striving. Take a moment and close your eyes. Do you see Him, lifting up the flap of His tent? A simple oasis in the midst of the ongoing, beckoning you to come. And when you do, you find that you are tucked not within a structure, but within His strength. Within the shadow of his wings. You breathe deeply of the sweetest scent, filling your lungs with the fragrance of His presence. It may be for a minute, an hour, or a whole day, but this is rest. And that rest is only found through Jesus. So as you go and do and conquer your slice of the world, don't neglect the moments when He calls you to come and be with Him.

Reflections

_____
_____
_____
_____
_____
_____
_____
_____

Month of:

Important This Week

-
-
-
-
-
-

Create ♡ Meal Ideas

Monday

morning

···
afternoon

···
evening

Tuesday

Create ♥ List it Out

morning

afternoon

evening

Milk & Honey
For Your Heart

"Then, because so many people were coming and going that they did not even have a chance to eat, he said to them, "Come with me by yourselves to a quiet place and get some rest."
Mark 6:31 NIV

Wednesday

Cultivate

morning

afternoon

evening

Mid-Week Reminder

Sabbath rest was not just meant for the Old Testament or for Jewish people. All of us who know Christ are to enter into that rest. To lay down striving to abide. In our modern culture it may seem impossible to set aside time to do so. But maybe if we break open the box of our perspective, we may find ways to incorporate rest as a rhythm instead of the exception.

Honest Thoughts

_____
_____
_____
_____
_____
_____
_____
_____
_____
_____
_____
_____

Thursday

morning

afternoon

evening

Friday

morning

afternoon

evening

Cultivate

REST

Saturday

☐ **morning**

• •
afternoon

Don't Forget to take time to Rest

• •
evening

Sunday

morning

afternoon

evening

Random Thoughts

WHERE/WHEN DO YOU HAVE YOUR BEST NAP?

Cultivate Prayer

Cultivate Gratitude

Create ♡ Notes & Hopes

WEEK 5 — Establish

"The Fig Tree"

"In the morning, as Jesus was returning to the city, He was hungry. Seeing a fig tree by the road, He went up to it but found nothing on it except leaves. "May you never bear fruit again!" He said. And immediately the tree withered."
Matthew 21:18-19

Jesus cursed the fig tree because it didn't produce fruit when he reached for it. This is not a statement of condemnation for us. We belong to Jesus. If we say that we are abiding in him and the Holy Spirit is within us, then there should be fruit that we are producing, even if that fruit is still within us, in season and out of season. In the physical, fruit is seasonal but in the Spirit, fruit is continual and overflows out of the Holy Spirit. We must decide that we will not hold back just because it is not the season for outward fruit. We must decide to cultivate what we have, steward it well and be ready to produce, to fight, to pray, to teach, to be…whenever we are called to. What fruit are you producing in this season?

Reflections

_____
_____
_____
_____
_____
_____
_____
_____
_____
_____

Month of:

Monday

☐ morning

Important This Week

- ⬡
- ⬡
- ⬡
- ⬡
- ⬡
- ⬡

•••••••••••••••••••••••••••
afternoon

Create ♡ Meal Ideas

•••••••••••••••••••••••••••
evening

Tuesday

morning

afternoon

evening

Create ♡ List it Out

○
○
○
○
○
○
○
○
○
○
○
○
○
○
○
○
○
○
○

Milk & Honey
For Your Heart

"Truly I tell you," Jesus replied, "if you have faith and do not doubt, not only will you do what was done to the fig tree, but even if you say to this mountain, 'Be lifted up and thrown into the sea,' it will happen. If you believe, you will receive whatever you ask in prayer."
Matthew 18:21 NIV

Wednesday

Cultivate

morning

afternoon

evening

Mid-Week Reminder

The art of cultivating is not in just picking the fruit that grows. It's in preparing the soil, planting the seeds, pouring in the water, getting positioned in the sun and trusting in the process that takes place to bring forth what needs to grow.

Honest Thoughts

_____
_____
_____
_____
_____
_____
_____
_____
_____
_____
_____
_____

Thursday

morning

afternoon

evening

Friday

morning

afternoon

evening

Cultivate
YOUR HEART

Saturday

morning

· ·
afternoon

Don't Forget to take time to Rest
· ·
evening

Sunday

morning

afternoon

evening

Random Thoughts
WHAT IS YOUR FAVORITE FRUIT/VEGETABLE?

Cultivate Prayer

Cultivate Gratitude

Create ♡ Notes & Hopes

"His Presence"

"If you are pleased with me, teach me your ways so I may know you and continue to find favor with you. Remember that this nation is your people." The Lord replied, "My Presence will go with you, and I will give you rest."
Exodus 33:13-14 NIV

Wasn't it Moses who said, if your presence doesn't go with us we do not want to go? This type of relationship doesn't settle for counterfeits. When you've tasted the reality of His presence anything less is sour and unsatisfying. The Lord called his people out of Egypt so that they could worship him. That was the goal. He brought plagues, and brought provision and did everything so that they would know Him, that is the essence of our worship, to know God and be known by Him. To encounter and remain in His presence. Is there a time that you experienced the tangible presence of the Lord?

Reflections

_____
_____
_____
_____
_____
_____
_____
_____
_____

Month of:

Important This Week

- ◯
- ◯
- ◯
- ◯
- ◯
- ◯

Create ♥ Meal Ideas

Monday

morning

• •
afternoon

• •
evening

Tuesday

Create ♡ List it Out

morning

afternoon

evening

Milk & Honey
FOR YOUR HEART

"JESUS SAID TO HER, "EVERYONE WHO DRINKS THIS WATER WILL BE THIRSTY AGAIN. BUT WHOEVER DRINKS THE WATER I GIVE HIM WILL NEVER THIRST. INDEED, THE WATER I GIVE HIM WILL BECOME IN HIM A FOUNT OF WATER SPRINGING UP TO ETERNAL LIFE."
JOHN 4:13 NIV

Wednesday

Cultivate

morning

afternoon

evening

Mid-Week Reminder

Jesus is our best investment. Without question. But as you think about John 4:13 you realize that Jesus also considers us a good investment. He has water for us to take in and drink of, refreshment that he is willing to pour into us. And when he does, he promises that this water will continue and not run dry, becoming a fountain in our own lives. Take a drink or a dip, sister, the water is fine.

Honest Thoughts

_____
_____
_____
_____
_____
_____
_____
_____
_____
_____
_____
_____
_____

Thursday

morning

·················· afternoon

·················· evening

Friday

morning

·················· afternoon

·················· evening

Cultivate
YOUR SEEKING

Saturday

morning

afternoon

Don't Forget to take time to Rest

evening

Sunday

morning

afternoon

evening

Random Thoughts

If you could choose one thing to splurge on, what would it be?

Cultivate Prayer

Cultivate Gratitude

Create ♡ Notes & Hopes

WEEK 17 — Establish

"Peace"

"What you have learned and received and heard and seen in me—practice these things, and the God of peace will be with you." **Philippians 4:9 ESV**

Peace is a word that is at times boxed in by our own definitions or perspective, maybe based on our own circumstances. What does it really mean to be at peace? How does it apply to our lives and the situations we find ourselves in from day to day? Is peace just our desire to finally be done with our household tasks? Or finally having a drama free day at work? Is it the beautiful landscapes that we are surrounded by or travel to visit? Immovable as mountains may seem? Standing for centuries and millennia yet can break, burst and flow with volcanic activity. I'm finding that peace is not necessarily stoic or a statue. It is calm amidst a storm and sometimes it is the storm itself. Bringing quiet to chaos or destruction to injustice. Setting right what has gone out of alignment and making way for rivers of living water. Peace moves and flows and waits, not dependent on us but led by the One who created it in the first place. The One who is actually peace itself. Peace does not always feel comfortable. Sometimes peace has to push its way into your grief, into your chaos, into your routine. Peace shouts peace and brings quiet. Peace speaks and makes way for life to flow. Is there a another perspective of peace the Lord has shown you?

Reflections

_____
_____
_____
_____
_____

Month of:

Important This Week

- ◯
- ◯
- ◯
- ◯
- ◯
- ◯

Create ♡ Meal Ideas

Monday

morning

....
afternoon

....
evening

Tuesday

Create ♡ List it Out

morning

afternoon

evening

Milk & Honey
For Your Heart

"He stilled the storm to a whisper; the waves of the sea were hushed. They were glad when it grew calm, and he guided them to their desired haven."
Psalm 107:29-30 NIV

Wednesday

Cultivate

morning

afternoon

evening

Mid-Week Reminder

Jesus be Prince of Peace over our lives, wherever we find ourselves. Break through our expectations, be the calm in the midst and be the force that throws any unsubmitted agendas out like a tidal wave. Be the peace in Philippians that surpasses our understanding and makes room for abundant kingdom living.

Honest Thoughts

_____
_____
_____
_____
_____
_____
_____
_____
_____
_____
_____
_____

Thursday

morning

afternoon

evening

Friday

morning

afternoon

evening

Cultivate

PEACE

Saturday

☐ **morning**

• •
afternoon

Don't Forget to take time to Rest

• •
evening

Sunday

morning

afternoon

evening

Random Thoughts

What creative things do you do to reduce stress?

Cultivate Prayer

Cultivate Gratitude

Create ♡ Notes & Hopes

WEEK 8 — Establish

"Worship"

"Mary then took a pound of very costly perfume of pure nard, and anointed the feet of Jesus and wiped His feet with her hair; and the house was filled with the fragrance of the perfume. John 12:3 NIV

When I know who I am in Christ and operate out of my identity and out of the overflow of intimacy with Him, the things I do are not just born out of my abilities. They are anointed supernaturally to bring shifts in the physical but also penetrate the spiritual realm. I believe it's the Lord's desire and it should be ours too, to not just bring physical change but for there to be eternal impact in what we do. As yourself, am I carrying an anointing that will affect my generations to come and the generations within my spheres of influence? Have I been around the Anointed One so much that what is on Him rubs off on me? When Mary poured the oil on Jesus, she worshiped so extravagantly, that the oil naturally remained on her too. The fragrance also spread to those in the room, her sphere of influence. They then had to come to grasp with their own surrender, their own worship or lack thereof. Her act released something to Jesus that automatically released back on her. It is the beauty of the abiding, the remaining. What does your lifestyle of worship look like?

Reflections

_____
_____
_____
_____
_____
_____

Month of:

Important This Week

-
-
-
-
-
-

Create ♥ Meal Ideas

Monday

☐ **morning**

••••••••••••••••••••••••••••
afternoon

••••••••••••••••••••••••••••
evening

Tuesday

Create ♡ List it Out

morning

afternoon

evening

Milk & Honey
FOR YOUR HEART

"WHILE THE KING WAS AT HIS TABLE, MY PERFUME SPREAD ITS FRAGRANCE."
SONG OF SOLOMON 1:12 NIV

Wednesday

Cultivate

morning

afternoon

evening

Mid-Week Reminder

When was the last time you did something out of the ordinary, unrehearsed, maybe a little over the top? I'm not talking about grabbing your favorite bottle of perfume and breaking it open. But would you consider the things in your life that you hold so dear to your heart? When you compare those things to the King of Kings are they worth holding on to so tightly? Who knows what God can do when you lay down what you love most in worship?

Honest Thoughts

_____
_____
_____
_____
_____
_____
_____
_____
_____
_____
_____
_____

Thursday

morning

afternoon

evening

Friday

morning

afternoon

evening

Cultivate
WORSHIP

Saturday

☐ **morning**

afternoon

Don't Forget to take time to Rest

evening

Sunday

morning

afternoon

evening

Random Thoughts

WHAT DO YOU THINK YOUR FINGERPRINT OF WORSHIP IS?

Cultivate Prayer

Cultivate Gratitude

Create ♡ Notes & Hopes

WEEK 9 — Establish

"Woman"

> "And who knows but that you have come to your royal position for such a time as this?"
> Esther 4:14b

Biblical womanhood is as varied as our fingerprints. Biblical women who God used were servants, queens, concubines, ex-prostitutes and former demoniacs. They were women who were married five times or never at all. They were little girls and pregnant teens. They were stay at home moms and moms who went to work. They were prophets and businesswomen, women with issues and women with none. They were orphans and widows, over-workers and those who worshiped extravagantly. We need to stop pointing the finger of comparison and remember that, along with men, we are called the Body of Christ, one that has many different parts and functions. We need to remember as we look in the mirror that our own bodies are not just the fingers and eyes and arms and legs and breasts and toes. But it's also our organs, our bones, our blood, our cells that make us who we are. The hidden parts do so much for the body that we can't even comprehend. We need to speak life and empowerment over each other and place a demand on the anointing on our sisters to be who they were created to be. How can you speak life and encouragement over another woman this week? (*Excerpt from Milk & Honey in the Land of Fire & Ice*)

Reflections

_____
_____
_____
_____
_____
_____

Month of:

Important This Week

- ◯
- ◯
- ◯
- ◯
- ◯
- ◯

Create ♡ Meal Ideas

Monday

morning

• •
afternoon

• •
evening

Tuesday

morning

afternoon

evening

Create ♡ List it Out

Milk & Honey
For Your Heart

"Kind words are like honey— sweet to the soul and healthy for the body."
Proverbs 16:24 NLT

Wednesday

Cultivate

morning

afternoon

evening

MID-WEEK REMINDER

Don't ever estimate how much your words and encouragement mean to others. In a culture where it seems profitable to tear someone down, to point out flaws and failures, we need more women who know how to build their sister up and speak the truth in love. The truth becomes much more real when you allow Jesus to give you eyes to see others the way He does.

Honest Thoughts

_____
_____
_____
_____
_____
_____
_____
_____
_____
_____
_____
_____
_____

Thursday

morning

afternoon

evening

Friday

morning

afternoon

evening

Cultivate
SISTERHOOD

Saturday

morning

afternoon

Don't Forget to take time to Rest

evening

Sunday

Cultivate Prayer

morning

afternoon

evening

Cultivate Gratitude

Random Thoughts

WHAT IS YOUR FAVORITE THING TO DO WITH FRIENDS?

Create ♡ Notes & Hopes

WEEK 20 *Establish*

"Seasons"

> "There is an appointed time for everything. And there is a time for every event under heaven. A time to give birth and a time to die; A time to plant and a time to uproot what is planted. A time to kill and a time to heal; A time to tear down and a time to build up. A time to weep and a time to laugh; A time to mourn and a time to dance. Ecclesiastes 3:1-4 NIV

Every single season matters and is part of the ebb and flow of life. Some are more comfortable than others but all are necessary. When we diminish someone's ability because they may be in a valley season or a wilderness season or maybe a work-at-home mom season or working full-time season or struggling with an issue season, whatever it is, we don't allow them to fully engage in what God is trying to do during that time. Remember that after God the Father declared who Jesus was during His baptism, the Holy Spirit is the one who led Jesus to the wilderness. What would that look like in this day and age? Would we think Jesus was struggling? Would we say that he was trying to isolate himself? He was led by the Holy Spirit into the wilderness to be tested and to encounter the love and provision of the Father. So when we discount where we are, we miss out on what God is trying to do in our lives right now. What treasures are in this season for you?

Reflections

_____
_____
_____
_____
_____
_____
_____
_____

Month of:

Important This Week

- ⬡
- ⬡
- ⬡
- ⬡
- ⬡
- ⬡

Create ♡ Meal Ideas

Monday

morning

•••••••••••••••••••••••••••
afternoon

•••••••••••••••••••••••••••
evening

Tuesday

Create ♡ List it Out

morning

afternoon

evening

Milk & Honey
For Your Heart

"Then Boaz said to Ruth, "Listen carefully, my daughter. Do not go to glean in another field; furthermore, do not go on from this one, but stay here with my maids. 9"Let your eyes be on the field which they reap, and go after them."
Ruth 2:8-9a NIV

Wednesday

Cultivate

morning

afternoon

evening

MID-WEEK REMINDER

Our preparation for the future is important but let us not get so focused on what is far ahead of us that we don't engage in and glean from where we are right now. Preparing in this way positions you for sweet surprises and promises that are waiting for you to discover.

Honest Thoughts

_____
_____
_____
_____
_____
_____
_____
_____
_____
_____
_____
_____
_____

Thursday

morning

•••••••••••••••••••••••••••••
afternoon

•••••••••••••••••••••••••••••
evening

Friday

morning

•••••••••••••••••••••••••••••••
afternoon

•••••••••••••••••••••••••••••••
evening

Cultivate
ENGAGEMENT

Saturday

☐ **morning**

• •
afternoon

Don't Forget to take time to Rest
• •
evening

Sunday

morning

afternoon

evening

Random Thoughts

WHO MAKES YOU LAUGH THE MOST?

Cultivate Prayer

Cultivate Gratitude

Create ♡ Notes & Hopes

WEEK 21 — Establish

"The Reward"

"But Samuel replied, "What is more pleasing to the LORD: your burnt offerings and sacrifices or your obedience to his voice? Listen! Obedience is better than sacrifice, and submission is better than offering the fat of rams.
1 Samuel 15:22 NLT

Every step we take in obedience moves us closer to the Lord. He is our reward. Many times we are looking for the incentive to obey. We are looking for what we can get in return. Blessings, more favor, more money, better health. And yes all these things are good and wonderful and needed. But we must be aligned, we must be in abiding. What does that look like? I think its good to go back to the beginning. What was the Lord's original intention? Looking back at Eden, at the garden, you see that it was relationship. Walking with the Lord. It wasn't even ministry. Even though that comes. It was relationship, it was God's breath in us. And from there Adam could name the animals. From there The Lord met a need in Adam's life that he didn't know he needed and brought Eve. We want favor in every area of our lives but what will you do with that Favor? The favor is not the reward, the Lord is. Jesus is.

Reflections

Month of:

Important This Week

- ◯
- ◯
- ◯
- ◯
- ◯
- ◯

Create ♡ Meal Ideas

Monday

☐ **morning**

• •
afternoon

• •
evening

Tuesday

Create ♡ List it Out

morning

afternoon

evening

Milk & Honey
For Your Heart

"Whatever you do, work at it with all your heart, as working for the Lord, not for human masters, 24since you know that you will receive an inheritance from the Lord as a reward. It is the Lord Christ you are serving."
Colossians 3:23-24 NIV

Wednesday

Cultivate

morning

afternoon

evening

Mid-Week Reminder

You may not receive applause or notoriety or fame. You may not get a pat on the back or affirmation for the faithful things you do. But you are noticed, by the only One who really matters. In the Bible, some of the most beautiful and profound statements came from the mouth of angels when they said to people, "You are precious to God" or "You are highly favored." Think about this. Heaven takes notice of what you do.

Honest Thoughts

_____
_____
_____
_____
_____
_____
_____
_____
_____
_____
_____
_____
_____

Thursday

morning

afternoon

evening

Friday

morning

afternoon

evening

Cultivate
YOUR INTENTIONS

Saturday

morning

afternoon

Don't Forget to take time to Rest

evening

Sunday

Cultivate Prayer

morning

afternoon

evening

Cultivate Gratitude

Random Thoughts

WHAT HELPS YOU STAY FOCUSED ON YOUR GOALS?

Create ♡ Notes & Hopes

WEEK 22 — Establish

"Your Voice"

"Finally, brothers and sisters, whatever is true, whatever is noble, whatever is right, whatever is pure, whatever is lovely, whatever is admirable--if anything is excellent or praiseworthy--think about such things." Philippians 4:8 NIV

What is your voice meant to do? Really? I'm not talking about how well you sing, your professionalism in communication or the dynamics of your speech. These are all areas that are significant in the release of a public message. But even in that, what is the core signature of the breath of God flowing in and through you? What is it that you are meant to release into the earth that melds and mingles with the sound that all of creation conveys? The worship, the serenade that is in response to the one who created it all? Influence starts with worship. Worship takes place within intimacy and intimacy is cultivated when your identity is established in Father God through Jesus Christ. What kind of influence you release is determined by what you are inspired and influenced by. You become what you behold, you release what you receive.

Reflections

_____
_____
_____
_____
_____
_____
_____
_____
_____

Month of:

Monday

morning

afternoon

evening

Important This Week

- ⬡
- ⬡
- ⬡
- ⬡
- ⬡
- ⬡

Create ♡ Meal Ideas

Tuesday

morning

afternoon

evening

Create ♡ List it Out

Milk & Honey
For Your Heart

"Do not conform to the pattern of this world, but be transformed by the renewing of your mind. Then you will be able to test and approve what God's will is--his good, pleasing and perfect will."
Romans 12:2 NIV

Wednesday

Cultivate

morning

afternoon

evening

MID-WEEK REMINDER

In a culture that is bombarded with images and messages set on influencing our perspective, we have to be intentional about what we take in. What you are meant to do on the earth doesn't have to be dictated by anyone else. If you feel overwhelmed by counterfeit messages, take time to set your gaze on Jesus and allow him to transform any struggling thoughts.

Honest Thoughts

Thursday

morning

•••••••••••••••••••••••••••••
afternoon

•••••••••••••••••••••••••••••
evening

Friday

morning

•••••••••••••••••••••••••••••
afternoon

•••••••••••••••••••••••••••••
evening

Cultivate
YOUR VOICE

Saturday

morning

•••••••••••••••••••••••••••••
afternoon

Don't Forget to take time to Rest
•••••••••••••••••••••••••••••
evening

Sunday

morning

afternoon

evening

Cultivate Prayer

Cultivate Gratitude

Random Thoughts

WHERE DO YOU FIND INSPIRATION?

Create ♡ Notes & Hopes

WEEK 23 *Establish*

"Influence"

> "But when you pray, go into your room, close the door and pray to your Father, who is unseen. Then your Father, who sees what is done in secret, will reward you."
> Matthew 6:6 NIV

Sometimes influence is not in our words but in our actions. Sometimes it's in moves so secret and undercover that no one knows where the ripple originated, just that change has come. Are we willing to be women who are not always seen but whose presence is felt? Who make moves in spirit and truth, influencing the generations in secret? Significance is in your DNA, in the way God formed you. And to know the you that He is for, you have to know Him. It is now, where you are in your sphere of influence, that you play a significant part. Yet there is also a bigger picture you are a piece of. We may never know the implications of our actions until we can see the big picture from heaven.

Reflections

_____
_____
_____
_____
_____
_____
_____
_____
_____

Month of:

Important This Week

-
-
-
-
-
-

Create ♥ Meal Ideas

Monday

□ morning

• •
afternoon

• •
evening

Tuesday

Create ♡ List it Out

morning

afternoon

evening

Milk & Honey
For Your Heart

"NOW FAITH IS CONFIDENCE IN WHAT WE HOPE FOR AND ASSURANCE ABOUT WHAT WE DO NOT SEE."
HEBREWS 11:1 NIV

Wednesday

Cultivate

morning

afternoon

evening

Mid-Week Reminder

Not everyone may see the things that you do, the choices that you make in the hidden places. Your consistency in serving, doing the dishes, working in integrity. But your God does. Those are the places where trust is built. Where faithfulness and bold faith is stirred up. These are the times when worship becomes more than a song you sing on Sunday and becomes a pleasing aroma that you release all week long.

Honest Thoughts

Thursday

morning

afternoon

evening

Friday

morning

afternoon

evening

Cultivate
INTEGRITY

Saturday

morning

....
afternoon

Don't Forget to take time to Rest
....
evening

Sunday

morning

afternoon

evening

Random Thoughts

DO YOU HAVE ANY HIDDEN TALENTS?

Cultivate Prayer

Cultivate Gratitude

Create ♡ Notes & Hopes

WEEK 24 — Establish

"Milk & Honey"

"And you will have enough goats' milk for yourself, your family, and your servant girls." Proverbs 27:27 NLT

When the Lord told Israel he was taking them to a land flowing with milk and honey it wasn't just about the natural provision. He was releasing a prophetic declaration about the kind of culture he was creating, about the kind of people he was empowering to defeat darkness, minister to his heart and to love as his very own. That is a promise we must go after even now. We are not just asking for the Lord's presence to fall on those of us who are asking and seeking and hungry. We must desire provision to flow into every area, into every home. We need the presence of the Lord to come that annihilates every enemy and gives food to even those who feel unworthy and unqualified to come and receive. In the book of Judges we see the story of two women who got to be living illustrations of the promises of God. Deborah and Jael's names mean Honey Bee and Mountain Goat respectively, the type of creatures who produce honey and milk. Their intertwined story of victory became a beautiful representation of what it can look like when Milk & Honey flows through the land and from the people of God. How do you think the Lord has positioned you to release beautiful influence all around you?

Reflections

_____
_____
_____
_____
_____
_____
_____

Month of:

Important This Week

-
-
-
-
-
-

Create ♥ Meal Ideas

Monday

☐ morning

• •
afternoon

• •
evening

Tuesday

Create ♡ List it Out

morning

afternoon

evening

- ○
- ○
- ○
- ○
- ○
- ○
- ○
- ○
- ○
- ○
- ○
- ○
- ○
- ○
- ○
- ○
- ○
- ○
- ○

Milk & Honey
For Your Heart

"How sweet are your words to my taste, sweeter than honey to my mouth!"
Psalm 119:103

Wednesday

Cultivate

morning

afternoon

evening

Mid-Week Reminder

In a culture that seeks for affirmation from every other source than the One who made them, we have been positioned to point to Jesus. Our lives can be living illustrations of God's glory, showing the world around us what it looks like to really believe, to trust, to love. Who has God put in your path even now that you can share sweet words of hope with?

Honest Thoughts

Thursday

morning

afternoon

evening

Friday

morning

afternoon

evening

Cultivate
MILK & HONEY

Saturday

☐ **morning**

• •
afternoon

Don't Forget to take time to Rest

• •
evening

Sunday

morning

afternoon

evening

Random Thoughts

WHAT IS ONE OF THE BEST GIFTS YOU HAVE RECEIVED?

Cultivate Prayer

Cultivate Gratitude

Create ♡ Notes & Hopes

WEEK 25 *Establish*

"The Light"

> "When Jesus spoke again to the people, he said, "I am the light of the world. Whoever follows me will never walk in darkness, but will have the light of life." John 8:12

Jesus is the light of the world. He is the hope for all nations, all people, of all ethnicities. Because of the Holy Spirit dwelling within us we get to be the messengers of this glorious promise. We get to be the flashlights pointing the way to Hope, reflecting the smile of our Heavenly Father. Beaming out the intention of his glorious plan into the darkest of places, into the most confusing times. Piercing with laser point precision generational curses and things that have held all of us back for so long. When we dig into the Word of God we shine the lamp of the Word at our feet, we see the places that we are. But there is also the promise for there to be light on our path to guide the way forward. Step by step, leap by leap, from glory to glory, into His loving arms.

Reflections

_____
_____
_____
_____
_____
_____
_____
_____

Month of:

Important This Week

- ◯
- ◯
- ◯
- ◯
- ◯
- ◯

Create ♡ Meal Ideas

Monday

morning

••••••••••••••••••••••••••••
afternoon

••••••••••••••••••••••••••••
evening

Tuesday

morning

afternoon

evening

Create ♡ List it Out

Milk & Honey
For Your Heart

"YOUR WORD IS A
LAMP FOR MY FEET,
A LIGHT ON MY PATH."
PSALM 119:105 NIV

Wednesday

Cultivate

morning

afternoon

evening

Mid-Week Reminder

Take a moment today to sit before the Lord. Open up your Bible to Psalm 119 and be reminded of the power of His word in your life. Let the Word of God begin to shine a light into dark places you may not have noticed before.
What is He revealing?

Honest Thoughts

_____
_____
_____
_____
_____
_____
_____
_____
_____
_____
_____
_____
_____

Thursday

morning

afternoon

evening

Friday

morning

afternoon

evening

Cultivate
YOUR INFLUENCE

Saturday

☐ **morning**

•••••••••••••••••••••••••••••••
afternoon

Don't Forget to take time to Rest
•••••••••••••••••••••••••••••••
evening

Sunday

morning

afternoon

evening

Cultivate Prayer

Cultivate Gratitude

Random Thoughts

WHERE DO YOU SEE YOURSELF IN A YEAR?

Create ♡ Notes & Hopes

WEEK 26 *Establish*

"Growth"

> "I keep asking that the God of our Lord Jesus Christ, the glorious Father, may give you the Spirit of wisdom and revelation, so that you may know him better."
> **Ephesians 1:17 NIV**

I hope that this Cultivational Planner has been a useful tool and resource for you over the past few months. As you look back over some of the devotionals, what week impacted you the most? Why? What is something new that has been cultivated in your life since you began?

Reflections

_____
_____
_____
_____
_____
_____
_____
_____
_____
_____
_____
_____
_____
_____
_____

Month of:

Important This Week

-
-
-
-
-
-

Create ♡ Meal Ideas

Monday

☐ morning

....
afternoon

....
evening

Tuesday

Create ♡ List it Out

morning

afternoon

evening

Milk & Honey
For Your Heart

"Delight yourself in the Lord and He will give you the desires of your heart."
Psalm 37:4 NIV

WEDNESDAY

Cultivate

morning

afternoon

evening

MID-WEEK REMINDER

What quote or song or verse have you heard lately that is reminding you to continue to seek and delight yourself in the Lord?

Honest Thoughts

_____
_____
_____
_____
_____
_____
_____
_____
_____
_____
_____
_____

Thursday | Friday

morning

morning

•••••••••••••••••••••••••••••• afternoon | afternoon ••••••••••••••••••••••••••••••

•••••••••••••••••••••••••••••• evening | evening ••••••••••••••••••••••••••••••

Cultivate
GROWTH

Saturday

morning

afternoon

Don't Forget to take time to Rest

evening

Sunday

morning

afternoon

evening

Random Thoughts

WHAT IS SOMETHING YOU ARE LOOKING FORWARD TO?

Cultivate Prayer

Cultivate Gratitude

Create ♡ Notes & Hopes

Creative Space

Creative Space

Creative Space

CULTIVATING SWEET SPOTS OF
CHRIST CENTERED IDENTITY, INTIMACY,
& INFLUENCE IN EVERY SEASON

Milk & Honey

In the Land of Fire & Ice

If you enjoyed this Cultivational Planner you will LOVE this latest book by Jenny!

About the Author

Jenny Erlingsson is wife to her amazing viking husband and mother to four cute and fierce mocha drops. After over twelve years of serving in pastoral ministry in Alabama, she and her family currently live in Iceland working in various areas of ministry. Jenny is passionate about empowering others, especially women through her writing and speaking. Along with the book **Milk & Honey in the Land of Fire & Ice**, she is also the author of the book **Becoming His: Finding Your Place as a Daughter of God**

www.ingramcontent.com/pod-product-compliance
Lightning Source LLC
Chambersburg PA
CBHW081228080526
44587CB00022B/3859